I0117474

John Dowland

The First Book of Songs, or, Airs of Four Parts with Tableture

for the Lute

John Dowland

The First Book of Songs, or, Airs of Four Parts with Tableture for the Lute

ISBN/EAN: 9783744676793

Printed in Europe, USA, Canada, Australia, Japan

Cover: Foto ©Thomas Meinert / pixelio.de

More available books at **www.hansebooks.com**

Ptolomeus

Marinus

DIRIGIT VVLNERE VERITAS

Aratus

Strabo

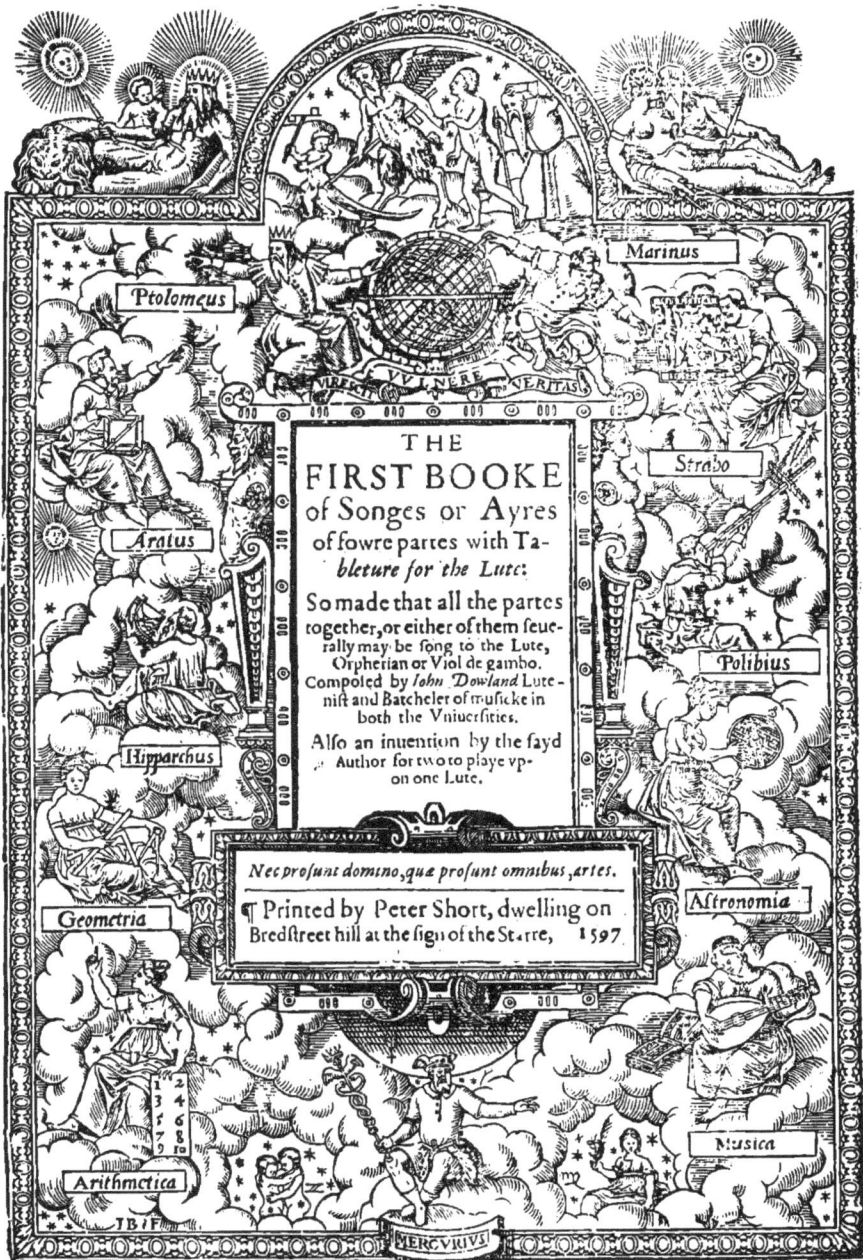

THE
FIRST BOOKE
of Songes or Ayres
of fowre partes with Ta-
bleture for the Lute:

So made that all the partes
together, or either of them seue-
rally may be song to the Lute,
Orpherian or Viol de gambo.
Compoſed by *Iohn Dowland* Lute-
niſt and Batcheler of muſicke in
both the Vniuerſities.

Alſo an inuention by the ſayd
Author for two to playe vpon one Lute.

Polibius

Hipparchus

Nec proſunt domino, quæ proſunt omnibus, artes.

❡ Printed by Peter Short, dwelling on
Bredſtreet hill at the ſign of the Starre, 1597

Geometria

Astronomia

Arithmetica

Musica

IB if

MERCVRIVS

COMME IE TREVVE

HONI SOIT QVI MAL Y PENSE

TO THE RIGHT HONOVRABLE SIR GEORGE CAREY, OF THE MOST HONORABLE ORDER OF THE GARTER KNIGHT:

Baron of Hunſdon, Captaine of her Maieſties gentlemen Penſioners,
Gouernor of the Iſle of Wight, Lieutenant of the countie of Southt.
Lord Chamberlaine of her Maieſties moſt Royall houſe, and of
her Highnes moſt honourable priuie Counſell.

T*HAT harmony (Right honorable) which is skilfullie expreſt by Inſtruments, albeit, by reaſon of the variety of number & proportion of it ſelfe, it eaſilie ſtirs vp the minds of the hearers to admiration & delight, yet for higher authoritie and power hath been euer worthily attributed to that kinde of Muſicke, which to the ſweetnes of inſtrument applies the liuely voice of man, expreſſing ſome worthy ſentence or excellent Poeme. Hence (as al antiquitie can witneſſe) firſt grew the heauenly Art of muſicke: for* Linus Orpheus *and the reſt, according to the number and time of their Poemes, firſt framed the numbers and times of muſick: So that* Plato *defines melody to conſiſt of harmony, number & wordes; harmony naked of it ſelfe: words the ornament of harmony; number the common friend & vniter of them both. This ſmall booke containing the conſent of ſpeaking harmony, ioyned with the moſt muſicall inſtrument the Lute, being my firſt labur, I haue preſumed to dedicate to your Lordſhip, who for your vertue & nobility are beſt able to protect it, and for your honourable fauors towards me, beſt deſeruing my duety and ſeruice. Beſides your noble inclination and loue to all good Artes, and namely the diuine ſcience of muſicke, doth challenge the patronage of all learning, then which no greater title can bee added to Nobilitie. Neither in theſe your honours may I let paſſe the dutifull remembrance of your vertuous Lady my honourable miſtris, whoſe ſingular graces towards me haue added ſpirit to my vnfortunate labours. What time and diligence I haue beſtowed in the ſearch of Muſicke, what trauel in forren countries, what ſucceſſe and eſtimation euen among ſtrangers I haue found, I leaue to the report of others. Yet all this in vaine were it not that your honorable hands haue vouchſaft to vphold my poore fortunes, which I now wholy recommend to your gratious protection, with theſe my firſt endeuors, humbly beſeeching you to accept and cheriſh thē with your continued fauours.*

Your Lordſhips moſt humble ſeruant,
Iohn Dowland.

To the courteous Reader.

HOW hard an enterprise it is in this skilfull and curious age to commit our private labours to the publike view, mine owne disabilitie, and others hard successe doe too well assure me: and were it not for that loue I beare to the true louers of musicke, I had concealde these my first fruits, which how they will thriue with your taste I know not, howsoeuer the greater part of them might haue been ripe inough by their age. The Courtly iudgement I hope will not be seuere against them, being it selfe a party, and those sweet springs of humanity (I meane our two famous Vniuersities) wil entertain them for his sake, whome they haue already grac't, and as it were enfranchisd in the ingenuous profession of Musicke, which from my childhoode I haue euer aymed at, sundry times leauing my natiue countrey, the better to attain so excellent a science. About sixteene yeeres past, I trauelled the chiefest parts of France, a nation furnisht with great variety of Musicke: But lately, being of a more confirmed iudgement, I bent my course toward the famous prouinces of Germany, where I founde both excellent masters, and most honorable Patrons of Musicke: Namely, those two miracles of this age for vertue and magnificence, *Henry Julio* Duke of *Brunswick*, and learned *Maritius Lantzgraue* of *Hessen*, of whose princely vertues and fauors towards me I can neuer speake sufficientlie. Neither can I forget the kindnes of *Alexandro Horologio*, a right learned master of Musicke, seruant to the royal Prince the *Lantzgraue* of *Hessen*, and *Gregorio Howet* Lutenist to the magnificent Duke of *Brunswick*, both whome I name as well for their loue to me, as also for their excellency in their faculties. Thus hauing spent some moneths in *Germany*, to my great admiration of that worthy country, I past ouer the Alpes into *Italy*, where I founde the Cities furnisht with all good Artes, but especiallie Musicke. What fauour and estimation I had in *Venice, Padua, Genoa, Ferrara, Florence*, & diuers other places I willingly suppresse, least I should any way seeme partiall in mine owne indeuours. Yet can I not dissemble the great content I found in the proferd amity of the most famous *Luca Mareuzio*, whose sundry letters I receiued from Rome, and one of them, because it is but short, I haue thought good to set downe, not thinking it any disgrace to be proud of the iudgement of so excellent a man.

Molto Magnifico Signior mio osseruandissimo.

PEr una lettera del Signior *Alberigo Maluezi* ho inteso quanto con cortese affetto si mostri desideroso di essermi congionto d'amicitia, doue infinitamente la ringratio di questo suo buon' animo, offerendomegli all' incontro se in alcuna cosa la posso seruire, poi che gli meriti delle sue infinite uirtù, & qualità meritano che ogni uno & me l'ammirino & osseruimo, & per fine di questo le bascio le mani. Di Roma à 13. di Luglio. 1595.

D. V. S. Affettionatissimo seruitore,
Luca Marenzio.

Not to ſtand to long vpon my trauels, I will onely name that worthy maiſter Giouanni Crochio Vicemaſter of the chappel of S. Marks in Venice, with whome I had familiar conference. And thus what experience I could gather abroad, I am now ready to practiſe at home, if I may but find encouragement in my firſt aſſaies. There haue bin diuers Lute leſſons of mine lately printed without my knowledge, falce and vnperfect, but I purpoſe ſhortly my ſelfe to ſet forth the choiſeſt of all my Leſſons in print, and alſo an introduction for fingering, with other books of Songs, whereof this is the firſt: and as this findes fauour with you, ſo ſhal I be affected to labor in the reſt. Farewell.

John Dowland.

Tho. Campiani Epigramma de
inſtituto Authoris.

Famam, poſteritas quam dedit Orpheo,
Dolandi melius Muſica dat ſibi,
Fugaces reprimens archetypis ſonos;
Quas & delitias præbuit auribus,
Ipſis conſpicuas luminibus facit.

A i

Nquiet thoughts your ciuill slaughter stint, & wrap your wrongs within à pensiue hart: And you my tongue that maks my mouth a minte, & stamps my thoughts to coyne them words by arte: Be still for if you euer doo the like, Ile cut the string, ij. that maks the hammer strike.

But what can staie my thoughts they may not start,   How shall I then gaze on my mistresse eies?
Or put my tongue in durance for to dye?   My thoughts must haue some vt els hart wil break,
When as these eies the keyes of mouth and harte   My tongue would rust as in my mouth it lies
Open the locke where all my loue doth lye;   If eyes and thoughts were free and that not speake.
Ile seale them vp within their lids for euer,   Speake then and tell the passions of desire
So thoughts & words and looks shall dye together,   Which turns mine eies to floods, my th oghts tofire

like, Ile cut the string, ij.   that makes the hammer strike.

and stamps my thoughts to coine them words by   art,   be still, ij.   for if you euer do the

a pensiue hart, and you my tonge that makes my mouth aminte, ij.

Nquiet thoughts, your ciuill slaughter stint,   and wrap your wrongs within

ALTVS.

BASSVS.

Nquiet thoughts, your ciuile

slaughters flint, and wrap your wrongs

within a pensiue hart, wrongs within a

pensiue hart, that makes my mouth amint

euer   to coine them words by arte,

do   the like, Ile cut y string, ij.

the string that makes y hamer strike.

TENOR.

Nquiet thoughts, your ciuile slaughter stint, and wrap your wrongs within a

pensiue hart, and you my tonge, my tonge that makes my mouth amint, and stampes my

thoughts, my thoughts, to coine, ij. them words by art, be still for if you euer do the   like

Ile cut the string, ij.   that makes the hammer strike.   A2

Ho euer thinks or hopes of loue for loue, or who belou'd in *Cupids*

lawes doth glorie, who ioyes in vowes or vowes not to remoue, who by this light-god

hath not ben made sorry: Let him see me ecclipsed from my son with darke clowdes of an

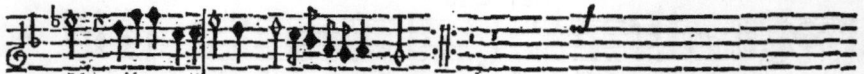

earth: ij.   Quite ouer   runne.

Who thinks that sorrowes felte, desires hidden,
Or humble faith in constant honor arm'd,
Can keepe loue from the friut that is forbidden,
Who thinks that change is by entreatie charm'd,
Looking on me let him know loues delights
Are treasures hid in caues, but kept by Sprights.

darke clouds of an earth. ij.   quite ouer run *Quite ouer runne.*

quite ouer runne with

Eclipsed from my son my son with

hath not bin made sorry : Let him see me. ij.

lawes doth glory. VVho ioies in vowes or vowes not to remoue, who by this light, God

Ho euer thinkes or hopes of loue for loue, or who belou'd in Cupids

ALTVS.

BASSVS.

Ho euer thinks or hopes of loue for loue

or who belou'd in Cupids lawes doth glory, who ioies in

vowes or vowes not to remoue, who by this light- god

hath not bin made sorry, Let him see me eclipsed from

my son, with darke clouds of an earth. ij

quite ouer runne, clouds of an earth quite ouer runne

let him see.

TENOR.

Ho euer thinks or hopes of loue for loue, or who be-　lou'd in Cupids

lawes doth glory, Who ioies in vowes or vowes not to remoue, who by this light-god

hath not bin made sorry, Let him see me eclipsed from my son, eclipsed frō my son with

darke clouds of an earth. ij.   quite ouer runne, of an earth, quite ouer run.

B.

Y thoughts are wingde with hops, my hops with loue, most loue vn- to

the moone in cleereſt night, and ſay as ſhe doth in the heauens

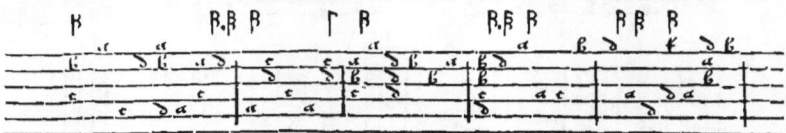

mooue   in earth ſo wanes & waxeth my de- light: And whiſper this but ſoftly

in her   cares,   hope oft doth hang the head, and truſt ſhed teares.

And you my thoughts that ſome miſtruſt do carry,   If ſhe for this, with cloudes do maske her eies,
If for miſtruſt my miſtriſſe do you blame,   And make the heauens darke with her diſdaine,
Say though you alter, yet you do not varry,   With windie ſighes diſperſe them in the skies,
As ſhe doth change, and yet remaine the ſame: Or with thy teares diſſolue them into raine;
Diſtruſt doth enter harts, but not infect,   Thoughts, hopes, & loue returne to me no more,
  And loue is ſweeteſt ſeaſned with ſuſpect.   Till *Cynthia* ſhine as ſhe hath done before.

in her eares, hope oft doth hang the head and truft thead teares:

heauens mooue, in earth fo wanes & waxeth my delight, & whifper this but foftly

vnto the moone, the moone in cleereft night, and fay as fhe doth in   the   the

Y thoughts are wingde with hopes my hopes with loue, mount loue

ALTVS.

BASSVS.

Y thoughts are wing'd with hopes my
hopes with loue, mount loue vnto the moone
in cleereft night, & fay as fhe doth in the heauens mooue, in earth fo wanes and waxeth
my delight, and whifper this but foftly
in her eares, her eares hope oft doth hang the
hed, and truft and truft thed teares,

TENOR.

Y thoughts are wingde with hopes my hopes with loue, mount loue

vnto the moone in cleereft night, and fay as fhe doth in the heauens mooue in

earth fo wanes fo wanes & waxeth my delight, & whifper this ij.   but foftly in

her eares, foftly in her eares, hope oft doth hang the head, and truft fhead teares·

B.2.

Can loue be ritch and yet I want,
Is loue my iudge and yet am I condemn'd?
Thou plenty haft, yet me doft fcant,
Thou made a god, and yet thy power contemn'd.
That I do liue it is thy power,
That I defire it is thy worth,

If loue doth make mens liues too fowre
Let me not loue, nor liue henceforth:
Die fhall my hopes, but not my faith,
That you that of my fall may hearers be
May here defpaire, which truly faith,
I was more true to loue, then loue to me.

hope in vaine,
fill complaine.

yet thou dost hope when I dispaire,
thou faild thou canst my harms repaire,

and when I hope thou makst thou makst me
yet for redresse thou leist thou leist me

O loue I liue   I liue and die in thee,   thy griefe in   my deepe sighs deepe sighs still speakes,
thy wounds do freshly freshly bleed in me,   thy vn-   kind vn- kind-nes breakes.

F my complaints could passions moue, or make loue see wherein I suffer wrong,
my passions were e-nough to proue, that my dispaires had gouernd me to long.

ALTVS.

BASSVS.

F my coplaints could passions moue,
my palsios were e-nough to proue,
or make loue see
wherein I suffer wrong,
that my dispaires had
gouernd me to long.
O loue I liue   and die in thee, thy griefe: ij.
Thy woûds do freshly bleed in me, my hart, iij.
in my deepe sighes still speakes,
for thy vn-kindnesse breakes,
and when I hope thou makst, ij,
yet forredresse thou leitt ij.
me
me
hope in vaine,
still complaine,

TENOR.

F my complaints could passions moue, could passions moue, or make loue see wherein I
my passions were e-nough to proue, e-nough to proue, that my dispaires had gouernd

suffer wrong,   O loue I liue   and die I liue and die in thee, thy griefe in   my deepe sighes
me to long.   thy wounds do freshly bleed do freshly bleed in me, my hart for   thy vn- kinde

deepesighes still speakes.   Yet thou dost hope when I dispaire, and when I hope thou makst mee
vn-kind-nes breakes.   thou faist thou canst my harmes repaire, yet for redresse thou letst me

hope in vaine,
still complaine.

An shee ex- cuse my wrongs with vertues cloake : Shall I call her
a re those cleere fiers which van- nish in to smoake: must I praise the

good when she proues vnkind,
leaues where no fruit I find.

No no where shadowes do for bo- dies stand, thou maist
Cold loue is like to words written on sand, or to

be abusde if thy sight be dime,
bubbles which on the wa- ter swim.

Wilt thou be thus a- bused still, seeing that

she will right thee neuer if thou canst not ore come her will, thy loue will be thus fruitles e- uer.

Was I so base that I might not aspire
Vnto those high ioyes which she houlds frō me,
As they are high so high is my desire,
If she this deny what can granted be.

If she will yeeld to that which reason is,
It is reasons will that loue should be iust,

Deare make me happie still by granting this,
Or cut of delayes if that dye I must.

Better a thousand times to dye
Then for to liue thus still tormented,
Deare but remember it was I
Who for thy sake did dye contented.

will thy loue will be thus fruitles euer.

be dim. Wilt thou be thus abused still, seeing that she will right thee neuer if thou canst not ore come her ter swim.

Cold loue is like to words writ like to words write on sande or to bubbles which on y water wa-

No no where shadowes do where shadowes do for bodies stand thou maist be abus'd abus'd if thy sight

are those cleer fiers which va-nish in to (smoake, must I praise y leaues where no fruit I find.

An she ex- cuse my wrongs with vertues cloake, shall I call her good when she proues vnkind,

ALTVS.

BASSVS.

An shee excuse excuse my wrongs with
are those cleer fiers cleer fiers which vanish
into smoake mult I praise y leaues where no fruit
vnkind, no no where shadowes do for bodies
I find, Cold loue is like to words written on
stand thou maist be abus'd if thy sight bee dimme.
sand, or to bubbles which on the water swimme.
Wilt thou be thus abused still, seeing that she will
right thee neuer if thou canst not come her,
will thy loue wil be thus fruitles euer

TENOR.

An shee excuse my wrongs, with vertues cloake, shall I call her good when she proues vnkind.
are those cleer fiers which va-nish into smoake, must I praise the leaues where no fiuit I find.

No no no where shadows do for bodies for bodies stand thou maist be abusd if thy sight thy sight
Cold loue loue is like to words to wordes written on sand or to bubbles which on the water wa-

be dim. Wilt thou be thus abused still, seeing that she will right thee ne- uer if thou canst not ore
ter swim.

come her will thy loue, will be thus fruitles euer,

Now O now I needs must part, parting though I obsent
while I liue I needs must loue, loue liues not when hope is

mourne, absence can no ioye em-   part, ioye once fled can not re -turne.
gone, now at last despayre doth proue, loue de- ui- ded lo- ueth none:

Sad dis- paire doth driue me hence, this dispaire vnkindnes sends.   If that

parting be   of- sence, it is she which then of-   fendes.

Deare when I from thee am gone,   Deare if I doe not returne,
Gone are all my ioyes at once,   Loue and I shall die togither,
I loued thee and thee alone   For my absence neuer mourne
In whose loue I ioyed once: Whom you might haue ioyed euer:
And although your sight I leaue,   Part we must though now I dye,
Sight wherein my ioyes doo lye   Die I doe to part with you,
Till that death do sence bereaue,   Him despayre doth cause to lie,
Neuer shall affection dye.   Who both liued and dieth true.

that parting be offence it is the which then offends.

prove, loue de-ui-ded loueth none.
part, ioy once fled can not returne.
Sad dispaire doth driue me hence, this dispaire vnkindnes sends, if

While I liue I needs mutt loue, loue liues not when hope is gone, now at latt despaire doth
Ow O now I needs mutt part, parting thought, abfent mourne, Abfence car no ioy em-

ALTVS.

BASSVS.

Ow O now I needs mutt part, parting
While I liue I needs mutt loue, loue liues
though I absence mourne, absence can no ioy em-
nor when hope is gone, now at latt despaire doth
Sad dispaire
part, ioy once fled cannot returne.
proue, loue de-ui-ded loueth none.
doth driue me hence, me hence, this dispaire vnkindnes sends. If that parting be offence it is the which
then offends.

TENOR.

Ow O now I needs must part, parting though I abfent mourne, absence can no ioy em-
While I liue I needs must loue, loue liues not when hope is gone, now at latt dispaire doth

part, ioy once fled can not return.
proue, loue de-ui-ded loueth none.
Sad dispaire doth driue me hence, this dispaire dispaire vnkindnes

fends. If that parting be of-   fence, it is fhe which then offends.

D

Deare if you cháge ile neuer chuſe againe, ſweete if you

ſhrinke Ile neuer thinke ofloue, Fayre if you faile,ile iudge all beauty vaine, wiſe if

to weake moe wits ile ne- uer proue. Deare, ſweete, faire, wiſe,change

ſhrinke nor be not weake, and on my faith, my faith ſhall ne- uer breake.

Earth with her flowers ſhall ſooner heau'n adorne,
Heauen her bright ſtars through earths dim globe ſhall moue,
Fire heate ſhall looſe and froſts of flames be borne,
Ayre made to ſhine as blacke as hell ſhall proue:
Earth,heauen,fire,ayre,the world transform'd ſhall vew,
E're I proue falſe to faith,or ſtrange to you.

TENOR.

nor bee not weake, and on my faith shall ne- uer breake.

neuer proue moe wits, ile ne- uer proue, Deare, sweet, faire, wise, ij. change, thrink

thinke of loue, faire if you faile ile iudge all beauty vaine, wise if to weake moe wits ile

Eare if you change ile neuer chuse againe, sweet if you thrink, you thrink ile neuer

BASSVS.

Ear if you change ile neuer chuse a- gaine, sweet if you shrinke, you shrinke ile ne- uer thinke of loue, faire if you faile ile iudge all bewty vaine, wise if to weake moe wits ile neuer proue, Deare, sweet, faire, wise, ij. change, shrink not be not weake, and on my faith, my faith shall neuer break.

ALTVS.

Eare if you change ile neuer chuse againe, sweet if you shrinke you shrinke ile neuer

thinke of loue, faire if you faile, you faile ile iudge all bewtie vaine, wise if to weake to weake

moe wits moe wits ile neuer proue, deare sweet. Deare, sweet, faire, wise, change, shrinke, nor be

not weake, and on my faith, ij. my faith shall neuer breake.

Burst forth my teares assist my forward griefe,
And shew what paine imperious loue prouokes:
Kind tender lambes lament loues scant reliefe,
and pine, since pensiue care my freedome yoaks.
O pine to see me pine ij. my tender flocks.

Sad pining care that neuer may haue peace,
At beauties gate in hope of pitty knocks:
But mercy sleeps while deepe disdaine encrease,
And beautie hope in her faire boosome yoaks,
O greiue to heare my grie se, my tender flocks.

Like to the windes my sighes haue winged beene,
Yet are my sighes and sutes repaide with mocks,
I pleade, yet she repineth at my teene:
O ruthles rigor harder the the rocks,
That both the Shephard kils, & his poore flocks?

ment ij. Loues scant re- liefe, And pine since pensiue care my fredom yokes ij.

paine ij.　imperious Loue prouoaks ij.　Kind tender lambes, la-

Vrst, burst forth my teares assist my forward greefe, And shewe what

ALTVS.

BASSVS.

Vrst forth: And shew what paine

imperious Loue ij.　prouoaks: Kind

tender lambs lament Loues scant reliefe,

and pine since pensiue care my fredom my

freedó yoaks, O pine to see me pine, to see me

pine my tender flocks.

TENOR.

Vrst, ij. forth my teares asist, asist my forward greif, And shew what paine, paine,

imperious Loue prouoaks: ij.　Kind tender lambes lament ij. Loues scant reliefe, re-

liefe, And pine since pensiue care, since pensiue care my free- dome yoakes, O pine to

see me pine, to see me pine, O pine to see me pine my tender flocks.

E.

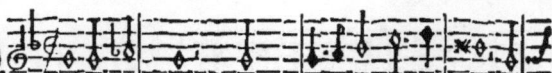

O cbriſtall teares, like   to the morning ſhowers, &

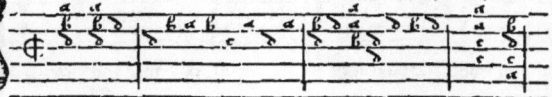

ſweetly weepe in to thy Ladies breſt,   and as the deawes reuiue the

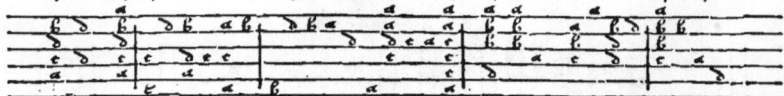

dropping flowers, ſo   let your drops of pittie be adreſt: To quicken vp   the thoughts

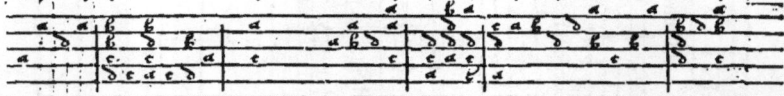

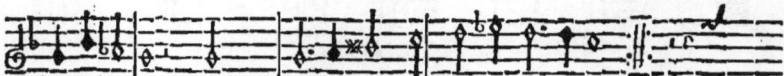

of my de-ſert,   which   ſleeps to ſound whilſt I from her departe.

Haſt hapleſſe ſighs and let your burning breath
Diſſolue the Ice of her indurate harte,
Whoſe froſen rigor like forgetfull death,
Feeles neuer any touch of my deſarte:
  Yet ſighs and teares to her I ſacryfiſe,
  Both from a ſpotles hart and pacient eyes.

whilst I from her, from her depart, from her depart. To quicken

pittie be adred, to quicken vp the thoughts of my desert, which sleepes too sound

to thy Ladies brest, & as the dewes reuiues the dropping flowers, so let your drops of

O chrisstall teares like to the morning flowers, and sweetly weepe in

ALTVS.

BASSVS.

O christall teares: And sweetlie weepe in to thy Ladyes brest, and as the deawes reuiue the dropping flowers, so let your drops of pittie be adrest; To quicken vp the thoughts of my desert, which sleeps too sound whilst I from her depart, from her departe;

TENOR.

O chrisstall teares like to the morning showers and sweetly weepe in

to thy Ladyes brest, and ij. as the deawes reuiue the drooping flowers, so let your

drops of pittie be adrest: to quicken vp the thoughts, the thoughts of my desert, which sleeps

too sound, whilst I from her, from her, departe, ij. from her departe, to quicken.

Hinkst thou then by thy fayning, sleepe with a proude
Or with thy craftie closing, thy cruell eyes

dis... playing, To driue me from thy sight, when sleepe yeelds more delight, such
...ceding, and while sleepe fayned lies, may not I steale a kisse, thy

harmles beauty gracing,
quiet armes embracing.

O that thy sleepe dissembled,
Were to a trance resembled,
Thy cruell eies deceiuing,
Of liuely sence bereauing:
Then should my loue require
Thy loues vnkind despite,
While fury triumpht bouldly
In beauties sweet disgrace.
   And liu'd in deepe embrace:
Of her that lou'de so couldly.

Should then my loue aspiring,
Forbidden ioyes desiring:
So farre exceede the duty
That vertue owes to beauty?
No, Loue seeke not thy blisse,
Beyond a simple kisse,
For such deceits are harmeles,
Yet kisse athousand fould,
   For kisses may be bould
When louely sleepe is armlesse.

ALTVS.

me from thy sight, when sleepe yeelds more delight, such harmlesse beautie gracing.
sleepe fained is, may not, I steale a kisse, thy quiet armes embracing?

Hinkst thou then by thy fai-ning sleepe with a proud disdaining,
Or with thy craftie clo-sing thy cru-ell eies reposing,
to drive
and while

BASSVS.

Hinkst thou then by thy faining,
Or with thy craftie closing,

to drive
and while

sleepe with a proude disdaining,
thy cru-ell eyes reposing,

me from thy sight, when sleepe yelds more de-
sleep fained is, may not I steale a

light, such harmles beautie gracing.
kisse, thy qui-et armes embracing.

TENOR.

Hinkst thou then by thy faining, sleepe with a proud disdaining, to drive me from thy
Or with thy craftie closing, thy cru-ell eyes reposing, & while sleepe fained

sight, when sleepe yeelds more delight, such harmeles beauty gracing.
is, may not I steale a kisse, thy qui-et armes embracing.

F

Come away, come sweet loue, The goulden morning breakes
All the earth, all the ayre Of loue and pleasure speakes,

Teach thine armes then to embrace, And sweet ro- — sie lips to kisse, And mixe our
Eies were made for beauties grace, Vewing ru- — ing Loue lóg pains, Procurd by

soules in mutuall blisse.
beauties rude dis-daine.

Come awaie come sweet loue,
The goulden morning wasts,
While the son from his sphere,
His fierie arrows casts:
Making all the shadowes flie,
Playing, staying in the groue,
To entertaine the stealth of loue,
Thither sweet loue let vs hie,
Flying, dying, in desire,
Wingd with sweet hopes and heau'nly fire.

Come away, come sweet loue,
Doe not in vaine adorne,
Beauties grace that should rise,
Like to the naked morne:
Lillies on the riuers side,
And faire Cyprian flowers new blowne,
Desire no beauties but their owne,
Ornament is nurce of pride,
Pleasure, measure, loues delight,
Haß then sweet loue our wished flight.

CANTVS *(inverted, top)*

to embrace, And ſweet roſie lips to kiſſe, And mixe our ſoules in mutuall bliſſe.
beauties grace,Vew- ing ru-ing Loue long paines,Procurd by beauties rude diſdaine.

ALTVS.

Ome away,come ſweet Loue,the goulden morning breakes.Teach thine armes then
All the earth all the aire, of Loue and pleaſure ſpeakes. Eies were made for

BASSVS.

Ome away,come ſweete Loue the
All theearth,all the ayre of

Teach thine
Eies were

goul-den morning breakes,
Loue and pleaſure ſpeakes,

armes then to embrace,
made for beauties grace,

And ſweet roſie
Vewing ruing

lips to kiſſe, And mixe our ſoules in
Loue long pains,Procurd by beauties

mutuall bliſſe.
rude diſdaine.

TENOR.

Ome awake,come ſweet loue, the goulden morning breakes.Teach thine armes then
All the earth,all the aire, of loue and pleaſure ſpeaks. Eies were made for

to embrace, And ſweete roſie lips to kiſſe,And mixe our ſoules in mutuall bliſſe.
beauties grace, Vew- ind ruing Loue lõg pains,Procurd by beauties rude diſdaine.

Est a while you cruell cares, be not more seuere thē
loue beauty kils & beautie spares, & sweet smiles sad sighs re-moue: *Laura*
fayre queen, of my delight, Come grāt me loue in loues de-spite, and if I euer faile to
honor thee: Let this heauen-ly sight I see, be as darke as hel to me.

If I speake my words want waite,
Am I mute, my hart doth breake,
If I sigh she feares deceit,
Sorrow then for me must speake:
Cruel, vnkind, with fauour view,
The wound that first was made by you:
And if my torments fained be,
  Let this heauenly light I see,
  Be as darke as hell to me.

Neuer houre of pleasing rest,
Shall reuiue my dying ghost,
Till my soule hath repossest,
The sweet hope which loue hath lost:
Laura redeeme the soule that dies,
By fury of thy murdering eies,
And if it proues vnkind to thee,
  Let this heauenly light I see,
  Be as darke as hell to me.

hea- uenly light I see, be as darke as hel to me.

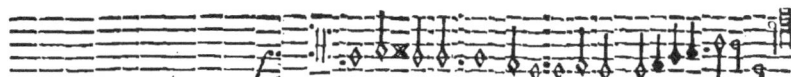

light,come grant me loue in loues de-fpite,and if I euer faile to honor thee, let this

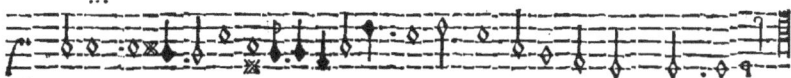

and beauty fpares,and fweet fmiles fad fighs re- moue, *Laura* faire queene of my de-

Eft a while you cruell cares, be not more feuere then loue, beauty kils

ALTVS.

BASSVS.

Eft a while you cruell cares, be not more feuere the loue, beauty kils & beauty fpares,& fweet fmiles fad fighs re-moue, *Laura* faire queen of my delight, come grant me loue in loues defpite,and if I euer faile to honour thee, let this heau'nly light I fee,be as darke as hell to me.

TENOR.

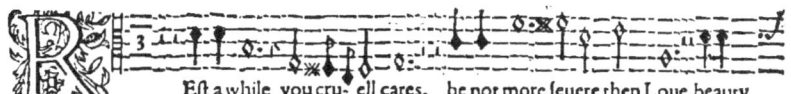

Eft a while you cru- ell cares, be not more feuere then Loue,beauty

kils and beauty fpares,and fweete fmiles fad fighes remoue, *Laura* faire queene of my

delight,come grant me loue,in loues de-fpite, and if I euer faile to honor thee,let this

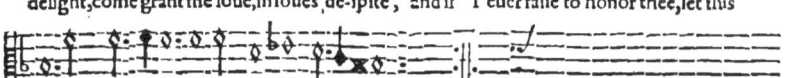

heau'nly light I fee, be as darke as hell to me.

G

Leep wayward thoughts, and rest you with my loue, Let not
Touch not proud hands, lest you her an- ger moue, But pine

my loue, be   with   my   loue   dif-   eafd.
yon with my   long-ings   long dif-   pleaf'd.   Thus wile she sleeps I sor-row for

her fake, So sleeps my loue, and   yet   my loue doth   wake.

But ô the fury of my restles feare,	My loue doth rage, and yet my loue doth rest,
The hidden anguish of my flesh desires,	Feare in my loue, and yet my loue secure,
The glories and the beauties that appeare,	Peace in my loue, and yet my loue opprest,
Between her browes neere *Cupids* closed fires	Impatient yet of perfect temprature,
Thus while she sleeps moues sighing for hir fake	Sleepe dainty loue, while I sigh for thv fake,
So sleepes my loue and yet my loue doth wake.	So sleepes my loue, and yet my loue doth wake.

loue difeafd,
long difpleafd,

Thus while fhe fleepes I forrow for her fake, fo fleepes my loue, ij. and yet

Leepe waiward thoughts,and reft you with   my loue, let not my loue be with my
Touch not proud handes, leaft you her an-   ger moue,but pine you with my longing,

ALTVS.

BASSVS.

Leepe waiward thoughts and reft you
Touch not proud handes leaft you

you with my loue, let not my loue be with my
her auger moue, but pine you with my longings

loue difeafd,
long difpleafd,

Thus while fhe fleepes I forrow for

her fake, fo fleepes my loue, fo fleepes my

loue, and yet my loue doth wake.

TENOR.

Leep waiward thoughts,and reft you with my loue, let not my loue be   with my loue
Touch not proud handes, leaft you her an-ger moue,But pine you with my longings long

difeafd,
ditpleafd,

Thus while fhe fleeps I forrow for her fake, fo fleeps my loue,   ij.   and yet ij.

my loue doth wake.

G 2

Care that consumes the heart with inward paine,
Paine that presents sad care in outward vew,
Both tyrant like enforce me to complaine,
But still in vaine, for none my plaints will rue,
Teares, sighes, and ceaseles cries alone I spend,
My woe wants comfort, and my sorrow end.

re- liefe,lend eares and teares, ij. ... to me moſt haples man, that ſings my ſorrowes

bliſſe but liue in griefe, are euermore delaid,All ye whole ſighs,ij. or ſickneſſe wants

Ll ye whom loue or fortune hath betraide,betraide,all yet that dream of

ALTVS.

BASSVS.

Ll ye whōloue or fortune hath

betraide,but liue in griefe, ye whole hopes

are euermore delaid, all ye whole ſighs

whole ſighs or ſicknes wants relief,lend ears

and teares, ij.

to me,ij.

moſt haples man,that ſings my ſorrows,my

ſorrowes like the dying Swan.

TENOR.

Ll ye whom loue or fortune hath betraide, All ye that dream of bliſſe

but liue in griefe,in grief,all ye whoſe hopes are eu- ermore,euermore delaid,delaid , all ye

whoſe ſighes or ſickneſſe wants reliefe, lend eares and teares to me,moſt haples man,moſt

haples man,that ſings my ſorrowes ſorrowes, my ſorrowes,like the dying ſwanne,

H

Ilt thou vnkind thus reaue me of my harte, ii.

and so leaue me: ii.   Farewell ii.   but yet or ere I part (O cruell) kisse me

sweete ii.   sweete my Iewell.

2
Hope by disdayne growes chereles
feare doth loue, loue doth feare,
    beautie pearcles.   Farewell.

4
Yet be thou mindfull euer,
heate from fire, fire from heat
    none can seuer. Farewell.

3
If no delayes can moue thee,
life shall dye, death shall liue
    stil to loue thee. Farewell.

5
True loue cannot be chainged,
though delight from desert
    be estranged.   Farewell.

ALTVS.

BASSVS.

Ilt thou vnkind thus reaue me of my heart, ij. and so leaue me, farewell, ij. but yet or ere I part (ô cruel) kisse me, ij. sweet my Iewel.

TENOR.

Ilt thou vnkind thus reaue me of my heart, ij. ij. and so leaue me, ij. farewell, ij. but yet or ere I part (ô cruell) kisse me, ii. sweet my Iewell.

Ould my conceit ÿ first enforſt my woe, or els
mine eyes which ſtill ÿ ſame encreaſe, might be extinct, to end my ſorrowes ſo
which nowe are ſuch as no-thing can releaſe: Whoſe life is death, whoſe
ſweet each change ofſowre and eke whoſe hell re-nu-eth euery houre.

Each houre amidſt the deepe of hell I frie,
Each houre I waſt and wither where I ſit,
But that ſweet houre wherein I wiſh to die,
My hope alas may not enioy it yet,
Whoſe hope is ſuch bereaued, of the bliſſe,
Which vnto all ſaue me allotted is.

To all ſaue me is free to liue or die,
To all ſaue me remaineth hap or hope,
But all perforce, I muſt abandon I,
Sith Fortune ſtill directs my hap a ſlope,
Wherefore to neither hap nor hope I truſt,
But to my thralles I yeeld, for ſo I muſt.

ALTVS.

BASSVS.

TENOR.

Come againe: sweet loue doth now enuite, thy graces that restraine, to do me due delight, to see, to heare, to touch, to kisse, to die, with thee againe in sweetest simpha- thy.

2
Come againe that I may ceafe to mourne,
Through thy vnkind difdaine,
For now left and forlorne:
I fit, I figh, I weepe, I faint, I die,
In deadly paine, and endles miferie.

1
All the day the fun that lends me fhine,
By frownes do caufe me pine,
And feeds me with delay:
Her fmiles, my fprings, that makes my ioies to (grow,
Her frowes the winters of my woe:

2
All the night, my fleepes are full of dreames,
My eies are full of ftreames,

My hart takes no delight:
To fee the fruits and ioies that fome do find,
And marke the ftormes are me afignd,

3
Out alas, my faith is euer true,
Yet will fhe neuer rue,
Nor yeeld me any grace:
Her eies of fire, her hart of flint is made,
Whom teares nor truth may once inuade.

4
Gentle loue draw forth thy wounding dart,
Thou canft not pearce her hart,
For I that do approue: (shafts
By fighs and teares more hote then are thy
Did tempt while fhe for triumps laughs.

doe me due delight,to see, to heare, to touch,to kisse,to die, ij. with thee againe in

Ome againe: sweet loue doth now inuite, thy gra- ces that refraine, to

ALTVS.

BASSVS.

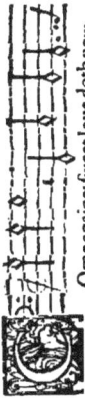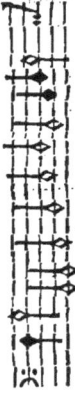

Ome againe: sweet loue doth now enuite, thy graces that refraine, to dome due delight,to see,to heare,to touch,to kisse to die, ij. with thee againe in sweetest simpathie.

TENOR.

Ome againe,sweet loue doth now enuite ,thy graces that refraine,to do me due

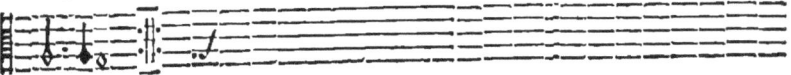

delight to see, to heare,to touch,to kisse,to die, ij. with thee againe, ij. in sweetest

fimpathie.

I 2

Is golden locks time hath to filuer turnde, O

time too fwift, O fwift- nes neuer ceafing,his youth gainft time & age hath euer fpurnd,

but fpurnd in vaine,youth waneth by en-creafing: Beautie,ftrength,youth are flowers

but fading feene, Duty, Faith, Loue are roots and euer greene.

His helmet now fhall make a hiue for bees,
And louers fonets turne to holy pfalmes:
A man at armes muft now ferue on his knees,
And feed on prayers which are ages almes,
But though from court to corage he departe
His faint is fure of his vnfpotted hart.

And when he faddeft fits in homely Cell,
Hele teach his fwaines this Caroll for a fonge,
Bleft be the harts that wifh my foueraigne well,
Curft be the foule that thinke her any wrong:
Goddes allow this aged man his right,
To be your beadfman now ý was your knight.

waineth, waineth, by encreasing, bewty, strength, youth, are flowers but fading seene, duty,

nes ne- uer ceasing, his youth gainst time and age hath e- uer spurnd, but spurnd, in vaine, youth

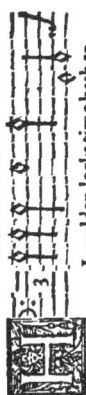

Is golden locks time hath to siluer to fil- uer turnd, O time to swift, O swift-

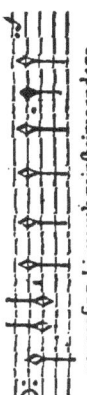

ALTVS.

BASSVS.

Is golden locks time hath to fil-uer turnd, O ime to swift, O swiftnes ne- uer ceasing, his youth gainst time and age hath euer spurnd, but spurnd in vaine, youth waineth by increasing; bewty, strength, youth are flowers but fading, seene, deuty, faith loue are roots and euer greene.

TENOR.

Is golden locks time hath to siluer turnd, O , O time to swift, ij. O swift-

nes neuer ceasing, his youth gainst time and age hath euer spurnd, but spurnd in vaine, youth

waineth by encreasing, bewty strength youth are flowers, but fading seene, deuty, faith, loue are

roots and e- uer greene.

K

Wake sweet loue thou art re-turnd, my hart which lóg in
absence mournd liues nowe in per-fect ioy,
only her selfe hath see-med
faire, she only I could loue, she one-ly draue me to
difpaire when she vnkind did proue.

Let loue which ne-uer ab-sent dies, now liue for e-uer
in her eyes when came my fiust a-noy,
difpayer did make me wish to
die that I my ioyes migyt end, she one-ly which did make
me flie my state may now a-mend.

If she esteeme thee now ought worth,
She will not grieue thy loue henceforth,
Which so difpaire hath proued,
Difpaire hath proued now in me,
That loue will not vnconstant be,
Though long in vaine I loued.

If she at last reward thy loue.
And all thy harmes repaire,
Thy happinesse will sweeter proue,
Raisde vp from deepe difpaire.
And if that now thou welcome be,
When thou with her dost meete,
She al this while but plaide with thee:
To make thy ioies more sweet.

loue, I could loue,ſhe onely draue me to diſpaire when ſhe vnkind did proue.
end,ioies might end,ſhe only which did mak me flie,my ſtate may now amend.

liues now,liues now in perfect ioy,   Only her felfe,her felfe hath ſeemed faire,ſhe onely I could
whence came,whence cae my firſt anoy,Diſpaire did make,did make me wiſh to die, that I my ioyes might

Wake ſweet loue thou art returnd,my hart which long in abſence mournd,
Let loue which ne- uer abſent dies,now liue for   e- uer in her eies,

ALTVS.

BASSVS.

Wake ſweet loue thou art returnd,
Let loue which ne- uer abſent dies,

my hart which long in abſence mournd, liues
now liue for   e- uer in her eies,whence

in perfect ioy,   Only her felfe hath
my firſt a-noy, Diſpaire did make me

nowe
came

ſeemed faire,ſhe onely I could loue,ſhe onely
wiſh to die,that my ioies might end,ſhe only

draue me to diſpaire, when ſhee vnkind did
which did make me flie,my ſtate may now a-

proue.
mend.

TENOR.

Wake ſweet loue thou art returnd,my hart which long in abſence mournd,liues
Let loue which ne- uer abſent dies,now liue for   e- uer in her   eyes,whence

now in perfect ioy,   Only her felfe,her felfe hath ſeemed faire,   ſhe only I could loue, ſhe only
came my firſt anoy, Diſpaire did make,did make me wiſh to die,   that I my ioies might end,ſhe only

draue me to diſpaire when ſhe vnkind did proue.
which did make me flie,my ſtate may now amend.

Ome heauy sleepe, ẙ Image of true death:

And close vp these my weary weeping eyes, whose spring of tears doth stop my

vitall breath, And tears my hart with sorrows sigh swoln crys: Com & posses my tired thoghts,

worne soule, that liuing dies, ij. ij. till thou one me bestoule.

Come shadow of my end: and shape of rest,
Alied to death, child to this black fast night,
Come thou and charme these rebels in my brest,
Whose waking fancies doth my mind affright.
O come sweet sleepe, come or I die for euer,
Come ere my last sleepe, coms or come neuer.

till thou one me once me befoule,

figh fwoln cries, Come and poffeffe my tired thoughts, worne foule that liuing dies, ij.

weeping eies, whofe fpring of teares doth ftop my vitall breath, and tears my hart with forrows

Ome heauy fleepe, the image of true death, and cloafe vp thefe my weary weary

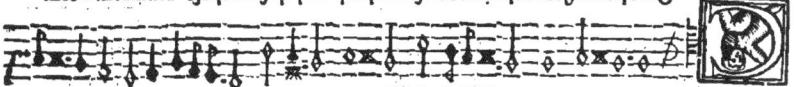

ALTVS.

BASSVS.

Ome heauy fleepe, the image of true death, and cloafe vp thefe my weary wee- ping eies, whofe fpring of teares doth ftop my vitall breath, and tears, ij. my hart with forrows figh fwoln cries, Come and pof- feffe my tired thoghts worn foule, y̆ liuing dies, ij. till thou, ij. on me, on me beftoule,

TENOR.

Ome heauy fleepe, heauy fleepe, the image of true death, and cloafe vp thefe,

my weary, ij. weeping eies, whofe fpring of teares doth ftop my vitall breath, & tears my

hart with forrows, figh fwolne cries, come and poffeffe my tyred thoughts worne foule, that

liuing dies ii. till thou one me one me beftoule.

L

Way with thefe felfe louing lads, whom *Cupids* arrowe
neuer glads. A- way poore foules that figh & weepe in loue of them that lie & fleepe, For
Cupid is a medooe god, & forceth none to kiffe the rod.

2
God *Cupids* fhaft like deftinie,
Doth either good or ill decree:
Defert is borne out of his bow,
Reward vpon his feet doth go,
    What fooles are they that haue not knowne
    That loue likes no lawes but his owne?

3
My fong they be of *Cyntihas* praife,
I weare her rings on hollidaies,
On euery tree I write her name,
And euery day I reade the fame:
    Where honor, *Cupids* riuall is,
    There miracles are feene of his:

4
If *Cinthia* craue her ring of me,
I blot her name out of the tree,
If doubt do darken things held deere,
Then well fare nothing once a yeere:
    For many run, but one muft win,
    Fooles only hedge the Cuckoo in.

5
The worth that worthineffe fhould moue
Is loue, which is the bowe of loue,
And loue as well the fofter can,
As can the mighty Noble-man:
    Sweet Saint, tis true you worthie be,
    Yet without loue nought worth to me.

poore foules that figh and weepe in loue of thofe that lye and fleepe; for *Cupid* is a medow

Way with thefe felfe louing lads, whom *Cupids* arrow neuer glads, away

ALTVS.

BASSVS.

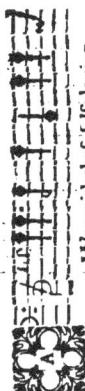

Way with thefe felfe louing lads whom *Cupids* arrow neuer glads, Away poore foules that figh and weepe in loue of thofe that lye and fleepe, for *Cupid* is a medow God, and forceth none to kiffe the rod.

TENOR.

Waie with thefe felfe louing lads, whom *Cupids* arrow neuer glads   A-

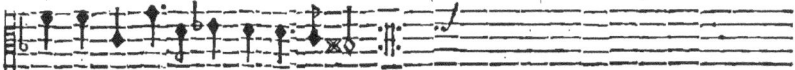

way poore foules that figh and weepe in loue, of thofe that lye and fleepe, for *Cupid* is a me-

dow god, and forceth none to kiffe the rod.

My Lord Chamberlaine his galliard.

www.ingramcontent.com/pod-product-compliance
Lightning Source LLC
Chambersburg PA
CBHW021554270326
41931CB00009B/1219